Fairy Garden Gathering

LINE ART COLORING PATTERNS

by Annie Lang

There's always something magical happening in Annie Lang's Fairy Garden and you are cordially invited to enjoy all the happy smiles with the many whimsical friends you'll discover within the pages in this enchanting publication. You'll find dozens of mix and match Fairy characters along with fantasy woodland cottages and themed wordart images to delight and inspire your creative spirit.

Simply trace the design and then transfer the image onto your project surface to make outstanding personalized items with professional results every time.

Copyright (C) Annie Lang 2020 anniethingspossible.com
The images in this book are intended for personal, classroom and small resale business use to create individually crafted items.   Use for the creation of commercially manufactured/printed product items is strictly prohibited. Content in this publication. may not be duplicated or distributed for the purpose of electronic data file sharing either for free or for profit. Annie Lang retains all rights to the copyrighted properties in this publication and rights to any images cannot be claimed, reassigned or transferred to another party.

Transferring the linework designs

Trace the design of your choice with pencil and tracing paper. Place transfer paper under the tracing paper and place onto your selected surface. Hold in place with tape if necessary. Retrace over the linework to transfer the design onto the project. For fabrics, trace the design, flip the pattern over and retrace the lines using a fabric transfer pen. Follow manufacturer's direction to iron the design onto your chosen fabric item.

Color or paint these designs with

Craft paints, watercolors, markers, coloring pencils, chalks, inks, fabric pens, paint pens, or crayons

These designs are great for

Home Dec Items like furniture, cabinets, accent items, walls, lamps, glassware, kitchen accessories, office and desk items, bathroom accents, cabinets, patio pots and outdoor items, etc. *Fabric and wearable items* like t-shirts, sweatshirts, aprons, canvas shoes, totes, quilting squares, table linens and napkins, window and shower curtains, pillows, etc. *Paper Craft Projects* like greeting cards, scrap page elements, tags, labels, stationery items, ornaments, gift bags, etc.

For more ideas and designer tips, please visit my Blog at

http://annielang-anniethingspossible.blogspot.com/ My Pinterest Board at http://www.pinterest.com/anniethings/ or my Facebook Page at http://www.facebook.com/anniethingspossible

Dream

Dream

Annie Lang's
Fairy Garden Gatherings

Copyright (C) Annie Lang

Copyright (C) Annie Lang

Copyright (C) Annie Lang

Annie Lang's
Fairy Garden Gatherings
Copyright (C) Annie Lang

Annie Lang's
Fairy Garden Gatherings
Copyright (C) Annie Lang

Copyright (C) Annie Lang

Annie Lang's
Fairy Garden
Gatherings

Annie Lang's
Fairy Garden
Gatherings
Copyright (C) Annie Lang

Annie Lang's
Fairy Garden
Gatherings
Copyright (C) Annie Lang

Annie Lang's
Fairy Garden
Gatherings
Copyright (C) Annie Lang

Annie Lang's
Fairy Garden
Gatherings

Copyright (C) Annie Lang

Copyright (C) Annie Lang

Annie Lang's
Fairy Garden
Gatherings

Annie Lang's
Fairy Garden Gatherings

Copyright (C) Annie Lang

Copyright (C) Annie Lang

Annie Lang's
Fairy Garden Gatherings
Copyright (C) Annie Lang

Annie Lang's
Fairy Garden Gatherings
Copyright (C) Annie Lang

Let there be Music
Let there be Music
wherever she goes
Music
wherever she goes
Annie Lang's
Fairy Garden
Gatherings
Copyright (C) Annie Lang

Annie Lang's
Fairy Garden
Gatherings
Copyright (C) Annie Lang

Faıry Garden

WELCOME

Annie Lang's
Fairy Garden
Gatherings

Copyright (C) Annie Lang

Annie Lang's
Fairy Garden Gatherings

Copyright (C) Annie Lang

Annie Lang's
Fairy Garden
Gatherings
Copyright (C) Annie Lang

Annie Lang's
Fairy Garden
Gatherings

Copyright (C) Annie Lang

Annie Lang's
Fairy Garden
Gatherings

Copyright (C) Annie Lang

imagine
Annie Lang's
Fairy Garden Gatherings
Copyright (C) Annie Lang
imagine

Annie Lang's
Fairy Garden Gatherings

Copyright (C) Annie Lang

Copyright (C) Annie Lang
Annie Lang's Fairy Garden Gatherings
Believe
Believe

Copyright (C) Annie Lang
Annie Lang's
Fairy Garden
Gatherings

Annie Lang's
Fairy Garden Gatherings

Copyright (C) Annie Lang

Copyright (C) Annie Lang
Annie Lang's
Fairy Garden
Gatherings

you don't always need
Wings
to fly
Annie Lang's
Fairy Garden Gatherings
Copyright (C) Annie Lang
you don't always need
Wings
to fly

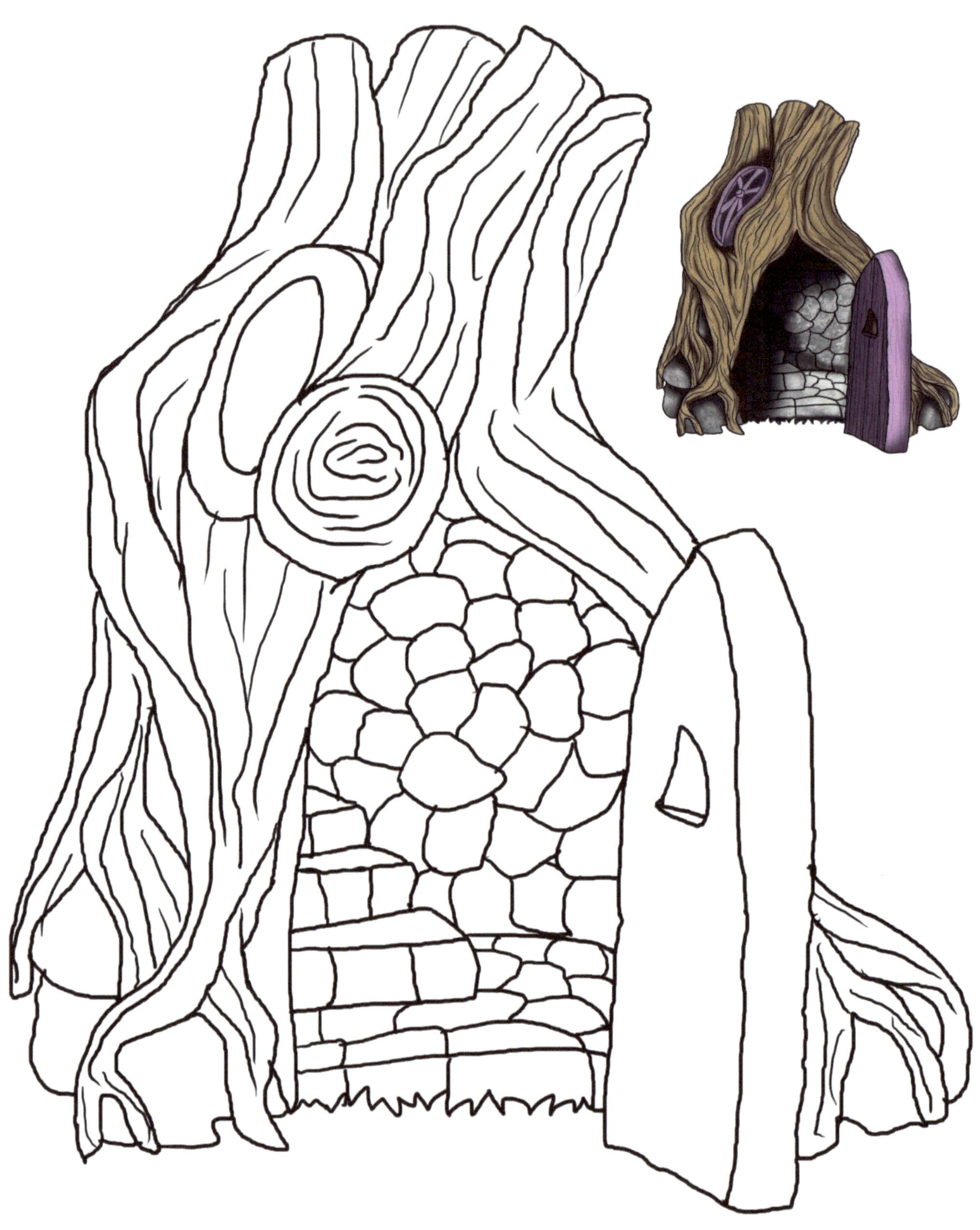

Copyright (C) Annie Lang **Annie Lang's Fairy Garden Gatherings**

Annie Lang's
Fairy Garden Gatherings
Copyright (C) Annie Lang

Annie Lang's
Fairy Garden
Gatherings

Copyright (C) Annie Lang

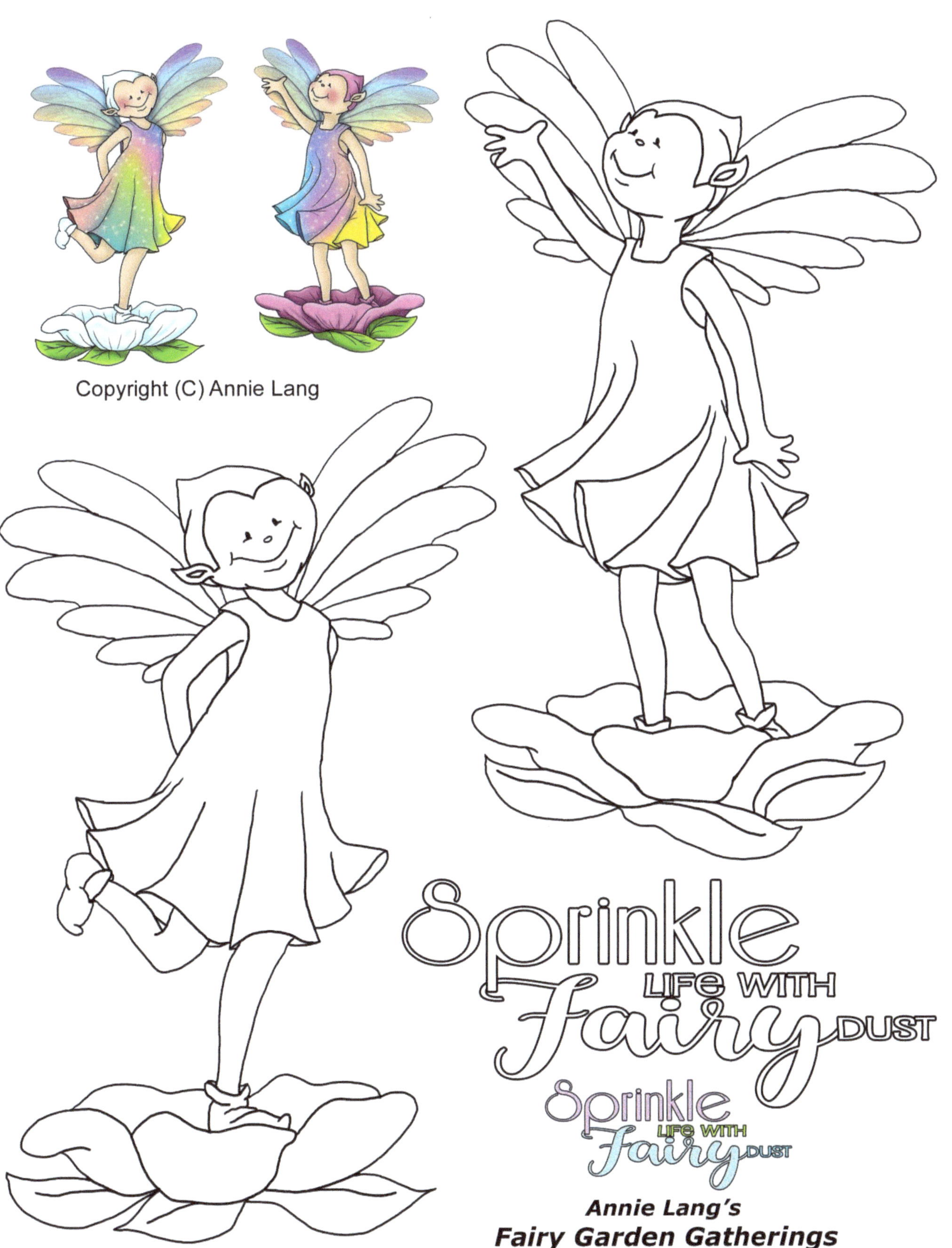

Copyright (C) Annie Lang
Sprinkle LIFE WITH Fairy DUST
Sprinkle LIFE WITH Fairy DUST
Annie Lang's
Fairy Garden Gatherings

Annie Lang's
Fairy Garden
Gatherings
Copyright (C) Annie Lang

Thank you for purchasing this publication!

Find dozens of other fun titles on my
Annie Lang's Books website!

I hope you enjoyed this book and
encourage you to leave a review and share your
thoughts for other customers at Amazon.com!

To learn more about the author, get free project
ideas, see video how-to's and more, please visit
Annie Lang's BLOG at
http://annielang-anniethingspossible.blogspot.com/

www.ingramcontent.com/pod-product-compliance
Lightning Source LLC
Chambersburg PA
CBHW040203240726
48664CB00002B/808